Living Love Forward

Through the Eyes of a Bully

A Children's Leadership Series

Written by Kim Dawson

Illustrated by Paige Anocibar

Copyright by Kim Dawson

Publisher: Tandem Services Press
PO Box 220, Yucaipa, CA 92399
www.tandemservicesink.com

Book Design by Paige Anocibar

ISBN 978-1-954986-22-0

Appreciation to

Inland Leaders Charter School and all our teachers and staff for inspiring and supporting me to write this series.

All my students and their families who taught me to be a better teacher and person.

The 2nd grade, 4th grade, and 5th grade classes at Inland Leaders and Wildwood that gave me GREAT feedback and helped me make this story better!

Pelican Elementary in Oregon for letting us use their school as a model for Lexie's Huckleberry Elementary.

My family and friends who have never wavered in supporting and encouraging my mission to help others.

Paige, my illustrator, for putting up with my "creative" tangents.

Jennifer Crosswhite, my editor and friend, who has been my sounding board and always keeps me positive when I hit the many bumps in the road.
(https://www.tandemservicesink.com)

All my readers who have supported me and helped me spread the message that kids can be leaders too.

Sending a ton of love and encouragement to all of you!
We got this!

From the author of the series Living Love Forward:

I wrote this children's leadership series to create an open conversation about the experiences our kids face every day. Being a teacher for over two decades, I have created connections with kids of all ages. I have observed and learned a lot through these interactions and have discovered key skill sets that I think are important for their growth. My purpose in writing these sentimental and caring stories is the hope that they instill life skills and resilience in our children. In turn, this empowers them to become successful and compassionate people, as well as strong leaders. Join Lexie and our children as they navigate this journey of self-discovery.

Please note that this series can be used in conjunction with any Leadership Program focused on survival skills and effective habits for children.

This book specifically focuses on:

- **Bullying**
- **Poor coping skills**
- **Poor self esteem**
- **Sadness**
- **Anxiety**
- **Disrespect**
- **Name calling**
- **Poor peer relationships**

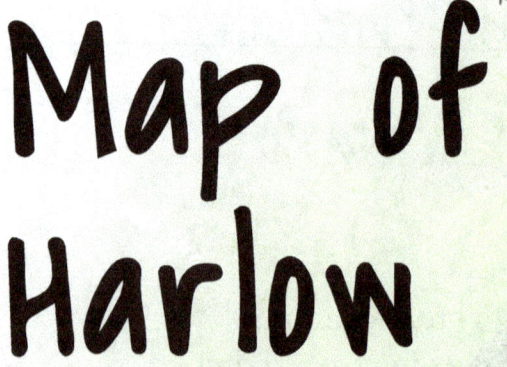

Map of Harlow

Train Station

Church Of Hope

Cemetery

Liberty Library

1st Street

2nd Street

3rd

4th Street

Rose Road

Daisy Lane

Lexie's House

Main Street

Bus Stop

Main Street

6th Str

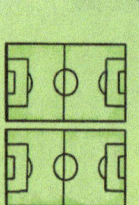

Jackson Sports Park

Lavendar Lane

Lotus Loop

Lavender Lane

Lavendar Lane

Jasmine Avenue

Jasmine Avenue

Jasmine Avenue

Riverside Park

Rose Road

Annabelle's House

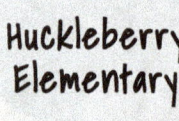

Huckleberry Elementary

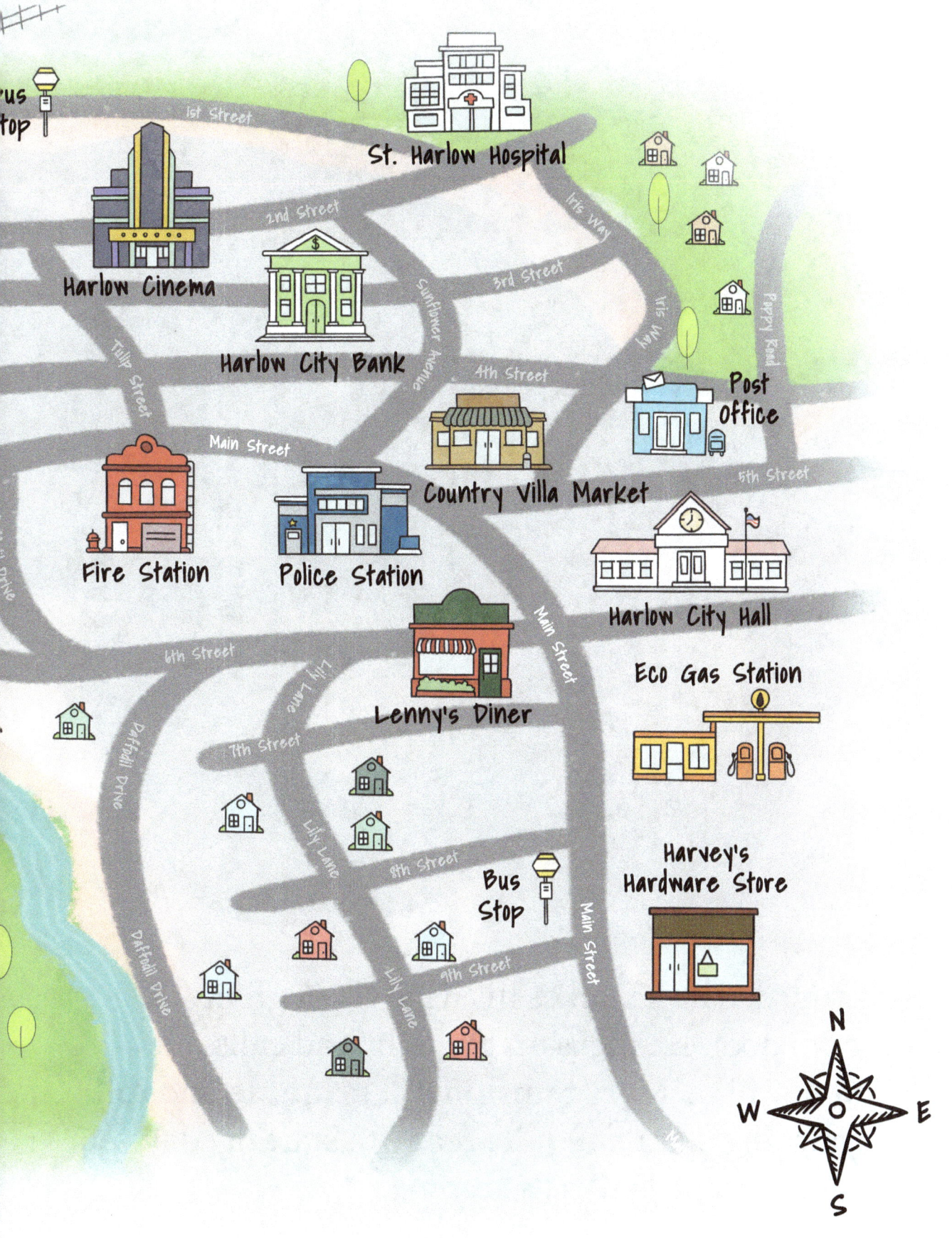

I hear my dad as he pokes his head through my
bedroom door. He flicks on the light and calls out,
"Good morning, Mary Sunshine!" I **grumble** and roll
over yawning. I am not quite ready to start my day yet.
Dad laughs as he leaves the room.

Slowly, I stretch and push myself up on my elbow to look out my window. There is a bird's nest in the tree just outside. I am hoping to see if the little babies are up yet.

"Nope! They must be sleeping in this morning," I say to myself as I swing my legs over and rise to start my day.

The weekend is almost here and that puts a pep in our step as my brother, Sam and I walk to school together. It's a good morning. That is until we round the corner and I see who is waiting at the school entrance.

Jason, the mean kid, is **perched** in his usual place on the "Welcome to Huckleberry Elementary School" sign. Like every morning, he is yelling mean comments to kids as they pass by.

I sigh, lift my chin up, and grab Sam's hand. We move quickly by hoping to go **unnoticed**.

You see, every Friday, I wear my grey hat to school. Jason and his buddies always have something to say about it. Luckily today, however, we slip right by him. Well, that is until we go out to recess.

A group of us, including my best friend Annabelle, are playing four-square when the wind kicks up, forcing my hat to sit **lopsided** on my head and I am careful not to let it fall off.

I end up playing four-square with one hand firmly on my hat while the other hand is free to **participate** in the game.

This is when Jason and his buddies come up and start harassing me.

"Look at the dummy wearing a hat!"

"Where did you get it...the dump?"

Jason walks right up to me and says loud enough for everyone to hear, "Why do you wear that dumb hat every Friday?"

I shrug and state in a strong voice, "Because every Friday, we used to go to my grandmother's for dinner. She died last year and gave me this hat to remember her."

I take a breath. When I continue I say, "She was a wise lady who taught me not to let people get under my skin. She said to smile sweetly and remind myself that their nastiness had more to do with how they're hurting. They may be feeling sad or angry inside. She said not to let anyone take my joy away."

Jason, surprised that I even spoke, was quiet for a moment. He could understand her missing her grandmother. About a year ago, his dad had passed away too. His dad had been in the Army and whenever Jason was missing him, he put on his dad's old Army jacket. He quietly mentions this to Lexie who nods with understanding.

I ask him, "What would your dad say to you right now if he was here? Would he want you to be mean to others just because you are upset?"

He thought for a moment. Frowning, he grumbles and walks away.

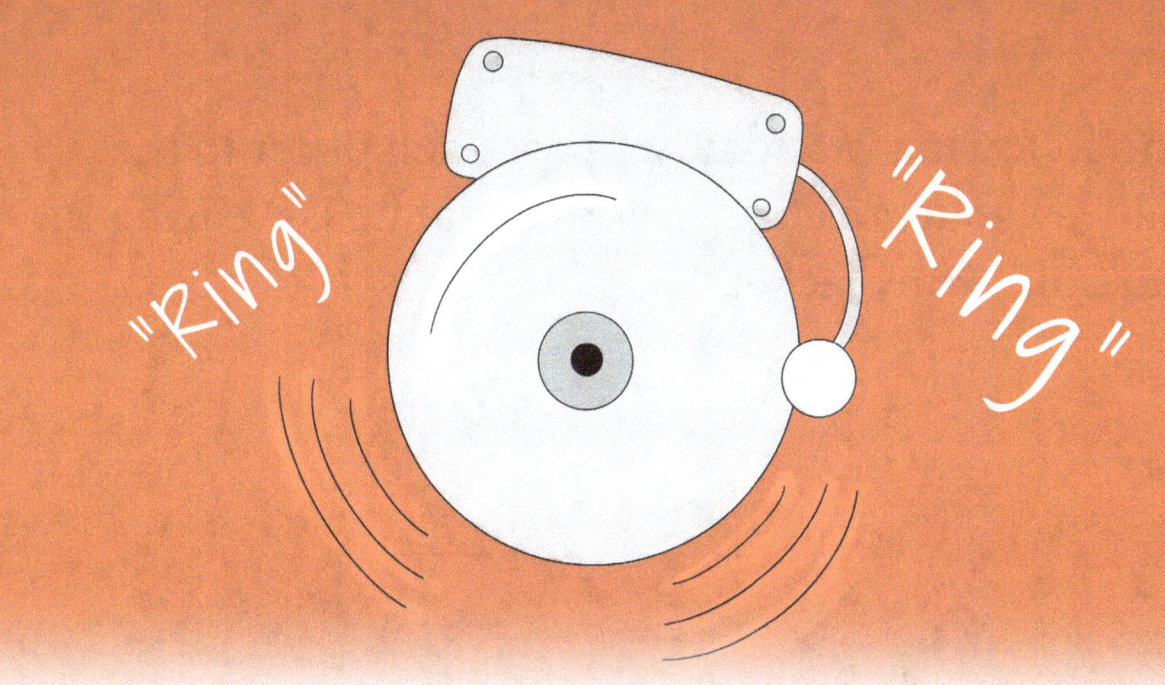

Just then the bell rings and the kids **scurry** to class. I didn't see Jason the rest of the day.

The following Monday, we pass each other in the hallway going to class. I notice that he is wearing his dad's old Army jacket.

He tucks his head slightly and softly says, "Hi" to me as we pass. I smile in return and continue on to class.

Author's Advice

* Don't let ANYONE take away your joy!

* Remember that their nastiness has more to do with how they're hurting.

* You never know what someone is going through so be patient and kind.

* Even if someone is hurting, it doesn't give them the right to hurt you.

Think and Feel

Look at page 7-8. Cover the words and look at the picture. Make up your own story based off of what you see rather then what the words are telling you. Be creative!

Glossary

grumble

Definition: to groan or mumble in a quiet, low voice; to complain; growl

Part of Speech:

This word is a (noun, adjective, **verb**, adverb).

Evidence of how the word is used in the story.

Lexie grumbles (groans and mumbles) when Dad wakes her up to go to school.

lopsided

Definition: crocked; uneven; leaning to one side

Part of Speech:

This word is a (noun, **adjective**, verb, adverb).

Evidence of how the word is used in the story.

The wind causes Lexie's hat to sit lopsided (leaning to one side) on her head while she is playing four-square.

Glossary

participate

Definition: to take part in; share in

Part of Speech:

This word is a (noun, adjective, **verb**, adverb).

Evidence of how the word is used in the story.

Lexie participates (takes part) in the four-square game at recess.

perched

Definition: A place to settle, sit or rest that is in some elevated position

Part of Speech:

This word is a (noun, adjective, **verb**, adverb).

Evidence of how the word is used in the story.

Jason, the mean boy, is perched (sitting) on the "Welcome to Huckleberry Elementary" sign while he picks on kids arriving to school.

Glossary

scurry

Definition: to go or move very quickly

Part of Speech:

This word is a (noun, adjective, **verb**, adverb).

Evidence of how the word is used in the story.

The kids scurry (walk quickly) to class so they will not be late.

unnoticed

Definition: not paid attention to; not seen

Part of Speech:

This word is a (noun, **adjective**, verb, adverb).

Evidence of how the word is used in the story.

Lexie and Sam go unnoticed (not seen) as they quickly walk by Jason.

About the Author: Kim Dawson

I am a single mom of two wonderful kids. I have been teaching for a number of decades and love spending time with my students. I have been writing since I was a child. It has always been a way for me to express myself when I am struggling. I strongly believe that we do not give our kids the credit they deserve. They have a lot to teach us if we just listen.

About the Illustrator: Paige Anocibar

Art is my passion. Every day I am thankful to have a career that empowers me to express myself through creativity. Drawing has been a part of my life since I was a small child. Coloring and painting were my favorite part of going to school. Back then, just like now, I was eager for the next art project. I knew that expressing myself through art is all I have ever wanted to do with my life, and illustrating this book has helped me achieve a part of that dream.

If you enjoyed this story, see other books in this Children's Leadership series, Living Love Forward.

2023 Books

February · May · September · November

2024 Books

February · May · September · November

www.ingramcontent.com/pod-product-compliance
Lightning Source LLC
Chambersburg PA
CBHW081014120626
46546CB00010B/3150